All About Energy

Harcourt

SCHOOL PUBLISHERS

Orlando   Austin   New York   San Diego   Toronto   London

Visit *The Learning Site!*

www.harcourtschool.com

Energy to Move

Cars move. People move. Think of all the ways you can move. You can move your arm. You can move your foot or your leg. You can move your whole body. You can move other people. Have you ever picked up a baby or rocked one to sleep? You move things, too. You pick up books. You throw balls. All this movement has one thing in common. It all takes energy! **Energy** is the ability to make something move or change.

This car moves very fast. It burns gasoline to get the energy to move.

Eating the right foods gives your body the energy to play soccer.

Cars get energy by burning gas. How do you get energy? You eat food. You eat breakfast before you leave for school. Your body changes the food you eat into energy. Your brain uses energy to pay attention and learn new things in math, science, and reading. Your muscles need energy so you can run and play and not get too tired. Without food, your body would not be able to produce energy for you to think, work, and play.

 MAIN IDEA AND DETAILS What is energy?

Different Kinds of Energy

People get their energy to move and grow from food. What about plants? Plants need energy, too. It takes energy for a seed to sprout. It takes energy for a tree or a carrot to grow. Plants make their own food by using the energy from the sun, from sunlight. Sunlight is a kind of energy called light energy. The main source of light energy on Earth is light from the sun. The sun also supplies heat. Most of the energy on Earth comes from the sun's heat and light.

These beautiful flowers need the sun to grow.

A siren on a fire truck is sound energy traveling away from it.

"R-r-r-i-i-i-n-n-g!" goes the telephone. "Honk" goes the car. You hear sounds all the time. You make sounds, too. But did you know that sound is energy? You have learned that energy is the ability to make something move or change. Sound energy is made when matter vibrates, or moves back and forth very fast. Sound energy travels away from the vibrating matter. When you hear something, it is because sound energy has reached your ears.

Light, heat, and sound are all different kinds of energy.

COMPARE AND CONTRAST How are heat and light energy the same as and different from sound energy?

Kinetic and Potential Energy

Energy can be grouped in two ways. **Kinetic energy** is the energy of motion. A rock rolling down a hill has kinetic energy. Without kinetic energy, that rock would stay at the top of the hill. It would not roll or move. Anything that is moving has kinetic energy. When you zoom down the street on a skateboard, you have kinetic energy. When a bird swoops in the sky, it has kinetic energy.

Think back to that rock at the top of the hill. Even before it started to move, it had energy. It had potential energy. **Potential energy** is energy of position. You can also think of potential energy as the energy that is stored in something. There is energy present, but it is not being used. Nothing is moving. Nothing is changing.

This turtle may be slow, but when it moves, it has kinetic energy.

This rock has potential energy now. If it starts to roll down the hill, the potential energy will change to kinetic energy.

A rock has potential energy and kinetic energy, but it does not have them at the same time. The rock at the top of the hill is not moving. Its energy is potential. The rock rolling down the hill is moving. Its energy is kinetic. When the rock began rolling, its potential energy became kinetic energy. When it stopped, that kinetic energy became potential energy.

 COMPARE AND CONTRAST When does an object have kinetic energy, and when does it have potential energy?

How We Use Energy

We could not live without energy. Plants need the energy from sunlight to grow. We need energy from food, and we get it from eating plants and animals. Food gives our muscles the energy they need to make our bodies move.

Machines use energy to move, too. Many machines get energy from combustion. **Combustion** is another word for burning. When we burn fuels, such as wood, coal, gas, and oil, heat energy is given off. Engines in cars, buses, trains, airplanes, and boats burn gasoline. The burning gasoline gives off energy. The energy makes the cars and other vehicles move.

Burning gasoline powers a car. There are different kinds of gasoline, but they all work in the same way.

There are many other uses for the heat that is released by combustion. Heat is used to cook food and boil water. It warms the air in our homes and other buildings during cold weather. Have you ever sat in front of a fireplace to get warm? If so, you have felt how burning wood gives off heat.

Heat released by combustion boils the water and cooks the eggs.

Heat is also produced when electricity is used. That is why lightbulbs become hot. Hair dryers use electricity to produce air warm enough to dry your hair.

MAIN IDEA AND DETAILS Why do you get warm when you stand in front of a fireplace?

We Need Energy!

You use energy in many ways. It takes energy for you to grow bigger and taller. It takes energy to walk and run and play. It even takes energy to sleep! When you are asleep, you are still breathing. Your heart is still beating. You use energy every moment of the day.

In a way, communities, towns, and cities are like people. Communities need energy every moment of the day. Every minute, even in the middle of the night, someone in the community is using energy. Someone is cooking; that takes energy. Someone has turned a light on; that takes energy. Others are driving their cars or using their computers or watching TV. All of these things take energy.

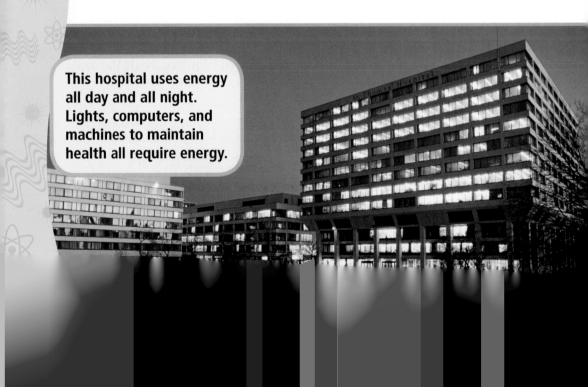

This hospital uses energy all day and all night. Lights, computers, and machines to maintain health all require energy.

Like other fossil fuels, oil is found under the surface of Earth.

Coal, oil, and natural gas are energy resources. We use coal, oil, and natural gas to release energy. A **resource** is something in nature that people use.

Coal, oil, and gas are called fossil fuels. **Fossil fuels** come from the remains of plants and animals that lived long ago. It took many years for fossil fuels to form.

 MAIN IDEA AND DETAILS What do people and communities have in common?

11

Renewable or Nonrenewable?

A resource that we cannot replace is called a **nonrenewable resource.** Fossil fuels are examples of nonrenewable resources. Every time we use fossil fuels, our supply of them gets smaller.

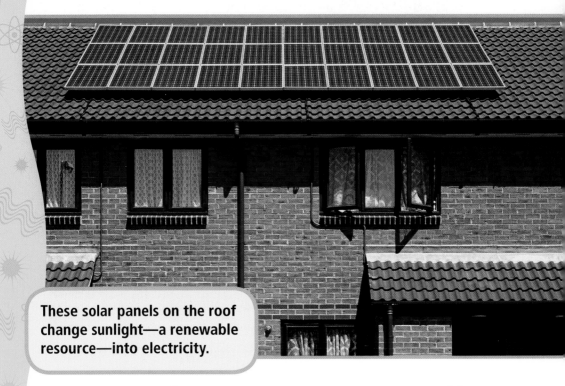

These solar panels on the roof change sunlight—a renewable resource—into electricity.

But not all energy sources are nonrenewable. A **renewable resource** is one that can be replaced. Energy from the wind is a renewable resource. Windmills can use wind to make electricity. Energy from the sun is also a renewable resource. The sun's energy can be used to make electricity. This electricity can be used to heat and cool buildings, to run computers, and to give us light.

Windmills use wind to make energy.

Think of all the ways you use energy. Think of all the ways your community uses energy. Think of how your community is growing. Each new building needs energy. Each new car needs energy. Each new person needs energy for living and working. Our nonrenewable resources could disappear. Scientists are always looking for more renewable resources.

⭐ **Focus Skill**

MAIN IDEA AND DETAILS Name some energy resources that are renewable. Name some that are nonrenewable.

Save Our Energy

Since we do not want our resources to run out, we need to try to save them. The easiest way to save energy is not to waste it. After you finish watching TV, turn it off. If you are the last person to leave a room, turn off the light. You can walk up the stairs instead of taking the elevator.

It takes energy to make all the things you use every day. So, if you reuse something, you save energy.

 MAIN IDEA AND DETAILS **What is one way a person can help save energy?**

No one is watching this TV. Energy is being wasted.

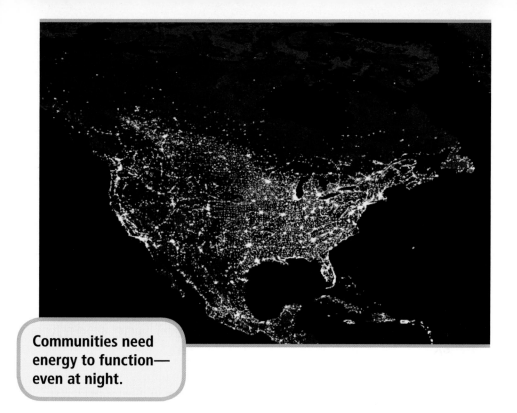

Communities need energy to function—even at night.

Summary

Energy is the ability to make something move or change. When something moves, it has kinetic energy. When something is not moving, it may have potential energy. Potential energy is energy of position or condition. People need energy to live. Communities need energy to function. Some energy resources, such as coal, oil, and gas, are fossil fuels. Fossil fuels are nonrenewable, which means that we cannot replace them. Other energy sources, such as wind and sunlight, are renewable. We can save energy by using less of it.

Glossary

combustion (kuhm•BUS•chuhn) Another word for burning (8, 9)

energy (EN•er•jee) The ability to make something move or change (2, 3, 4, 5, 6, 7, 8, 9, 10, 11, 12, 13, 14, 15)

fossil fuels (FAHS•uhl FYOO•uhl) A resource that comes from the remains of plants and animals that lived long ago (11, 12, 15)

kinetic energy (kih•NET•ik EN•er•jee) The energy of motion (6, 7, 15)

nonrenewable resource (nahn•rih•NOO•uh•buhl REE•sawrs) A resource that cannot be replaced before more can be made (12, 13, 15)

potential energy (poh•TEN•shuhl EN•er•jee) Energy due to position or condition (6, 7, 15)

renewable resource (rih•NOO•uh•buhl REE•sawrs) A resource that can be replaced quickly (12, 14, 15)

resource (REE•sawrs) A material that is found in nature and that is used by living things (11, 12, 13, 14, 15)